BACKYARD WILDLIFE

Skunks

by Emily Green

BELLWETHER MEDIA · MINNEAPOLIS, MN

Note to Librarians, Teachers, and Parents:

Blastoff! Readers are carefully developed by literacy experts and combine standards-based content with developmentally appropriate text.

Level 1 provides the most support through repetition of high-frequency words, light text, predictable sentence patterns, and strong visual support.

Level 2 offers early readers a bit more challenge through varied simple sentences, increased text load, and less repetition of high-frequency words.

Level 3 advances early-fluent readers toward fluency through increased text and concept load, less reliance on visuals, longer sentences, and more literary language.

Level 4 builds reading stamina by providing more text per page, increased use of punctuation, greater variation in sentence patterns, and increasingly challenging vocabulary.

Level 5 encourages children to move from "learning to read" to "reading to learn" by providing even more text, varied writing styles, and less familiar topics.

Whichever book is right for your reader, Blastoff! Readers are the perfect books to build confidence and encourage a love of reading that will last a lifetime!

This edition first published in 2011 by Bellwether Media, Inc.

No part of this publication may be reproduced in whole or in part without written permission of the publisher. For information regarding permission, write to Bellwether Media, Inc., Attention: Permissions Department, 5357 Penn Avenue South, Minneapolis, MN 55419.

Library of Congress Cataloging-in-Publication Data
Green, Emily K., 1966–
  Skunks / by Emily Green.
    p. cm. – (Blastoff! readers: Backyard wildlife)
  Includes bibliographical references and index.
  Summary: "Developed by literacy experts for students in kindergarten through grade three, this book introduces skunks to young readers through leveled text and related photos"–Provided by publisher.
  ISBN 978-1-60014-445-5 (hardcover : alk. paper)
  I. Title.
  QL737.C248G74 2010
  599.76'8–dc22   2010006444

Printed in the United States of America, North Mankato, MN.
080110   1162

Contents

Skunks are small animals that have black-and-white fur.

Most skunks have
two white stripes.
Some skunks
have many stripes
or spots.

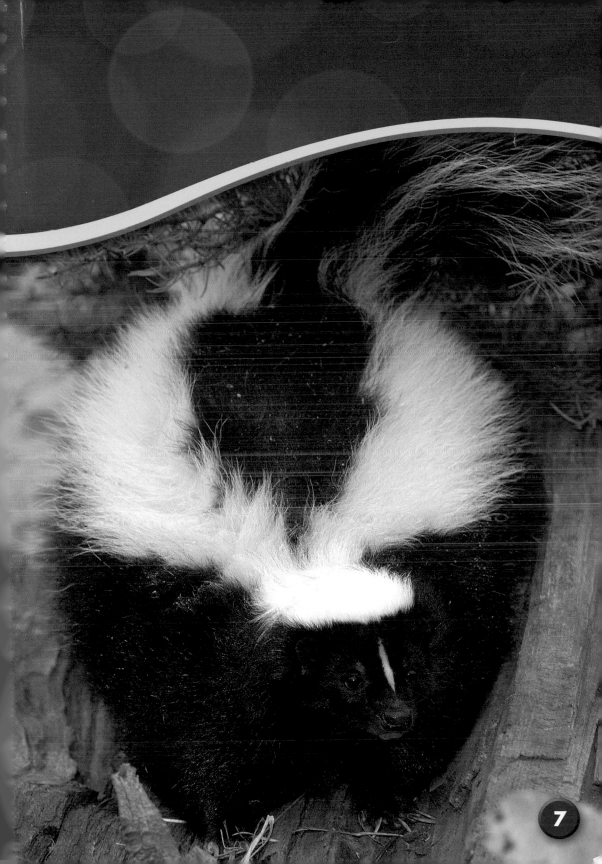

All skunks have
long, bushy tails.

Most skunks sleep
during the day.
They look for
food at night.

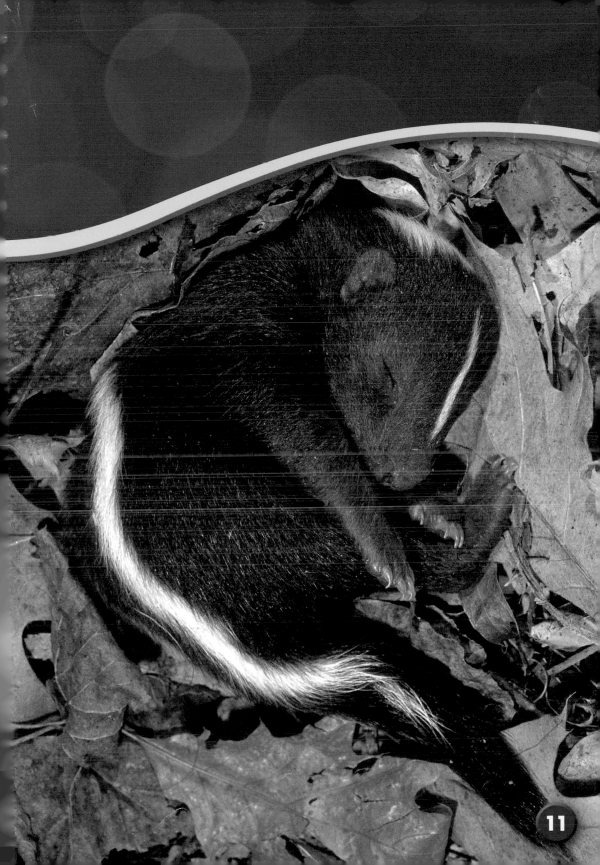

Skunks eat fruits, plants, and small animals. They dig small holes to find **insects**.

Skunks live in forests and fields. They make homes in hollow logs.

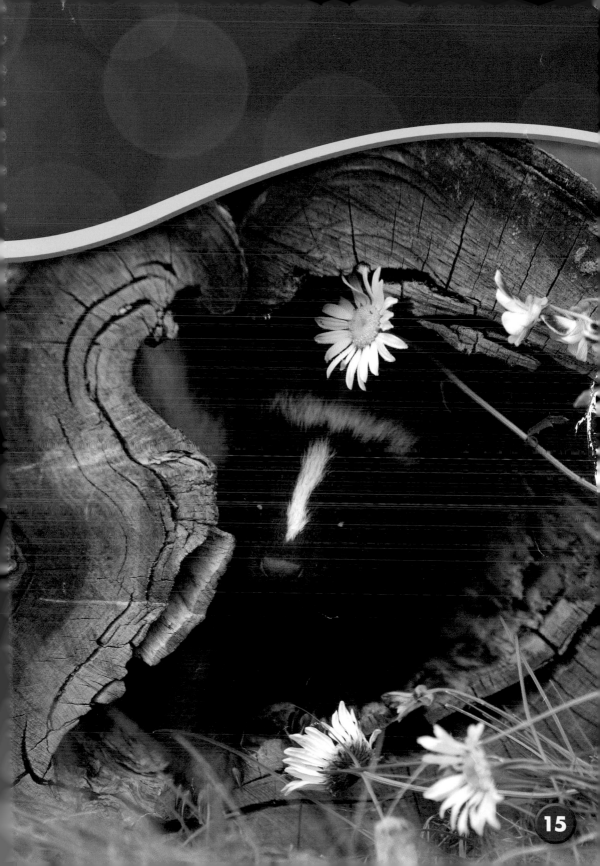

Some skunks live in cities. They look for food in trash cans.

Skunks like to be alone. They **growl** or **hiss** to scare away animals and people.

Skunks also **spray** a stinky **liquid**. They can spray six times in a row. Watch out fox!

21

Glossary

growl—to make a deep, angry noise

hiss—to make a long "S" sound

insects—small animals with six legs and hard outer bodies; insect bodies are divided into three parts.

liquid—something that can flow like water

spray—to shoot a liquid through the air; when a liquid is sprayed, it flies through the air in little drops.

To Learn More

AT THE LIBRARY

Newman, Lesléa. *Skunk's Spring Surprise*. San Diego, Calif.: Harcourt, 2007.

Otfinoski, Steven. *Skunks*. New York, N.Y.: Marshall Cavendish, 2008.

Souza, D.M. *Skunks Do More Than Stink*. Brookfield, Conn.: Millbrook Press, 2002.

ON THE WEB

Learning more about skunks is as easy as 1, 2, 3.

1. Go to www.factsurfer.com.

2. Enter "skunks" into the search box.

3. Click the "Surf" button and you will see a list of related Web sites.

With factsurfer.com, finding more information is just a click away.

Index

The images in this book are reproduced through the courtesy of: ARCO/R. Wittek/Age Fotostock, front cover; Minden Pictures/Masterfile, p. 5; Don Johnston/Photolibrary, p. 7; Corbis/Photolibrary, p. 9; Wayne Lynch/Photolibrary, p. 11; Robert Lubeck/Animals Animals – Earth Scenes, p. 13; Pinchuk Alexey, p. 13 (left); Graham Taylor, p. 13 (middle); Juan Martinez, p. 13 (right); Bruce Lichtenberger/Photolibrary, p. 15; Thomas Kitchin & Vict/Age Fotostock, p. 17; Holly Kuchera, p. 19; Animals Animals – Earth Scenes, p. 21.